Who Is the Holy Spirit?

FOSTER R. McCURLEY
JANNINE B. McCURLEY

BASIC QUESTIONS

Augsburg Fortress, Minneapolis

Contents

BASIC QUESTIONS
Who Is the Holy Spirit? Learner Book
This learner book has a corresponding leader guide.

Editors: Mark Gardner, Lynn Joyce Hunter, and Julie Lindesmith
Series design: Lois Stanfield, LightSource Images
Cover and interior art: Greg Lewis Studios

ISBN 0-8066-3819-2

Manufactured in U.S.A.
1 2 3 4 5 6 7 8 9 0 1 2 3 4 5 6 7 8 9

The Breath of Life

*God creates life in us and
so identifies us as beings totally
dependent on God.*

GENESIS 2:4b-25
THE FIRST HUMANS

The first human God created, according to the Bible, was named Adam. Adam's story might be the story of each and every one of us. It might be mine; it might be yours. If it is, the story has something important to tell us about God and ourselves.

Before Adam came into being, there was only dry sand, according to Genesis 2. What a bleak scene in which to begin our story! Yet the Lord God was as busy in that sand as a young child at the beach. In the bright sun, God pushed sand together to form what appeared to be a small tree trunk lying on the ground, then fanned out two roots and spread out just two branches. At the top of the trunk, God added an oval figure, pushed and formed valleys and elevations, making two eyes and a mouth and a nose.

So far, the story does not sound like yours or mine. It does not describe how we came into existence. The author would undoubtedly fail the exam in biology, even at the elementary school level. The author knew better, of course, and was complete-ly aware of the way people are born into life. That knowledge would be demonstrated in the description of Cain and Abel's births only two chapters later.

Far from writing about how we are born in this story, this author is driving at something much more important. The author wants us to understand to whom we owe life and who we are.

With those purposes in mind, the biblical storyteller writes that the Lord God "breathed into his nostrils the breath of life; and the man became a living being" (Genesis 2:7). It is God who breathes the breath of life into Adam, and so Adam will not be able to lift his newly formed body off the ground without realizing that he owes his very being to God. Without God's breath, Adam would have remained only a lifeless figure of sand to be swept away grain after grain by the next strong breeze. With God's breath, Adam came alive to be who God created him to be.

In this course about the Holy Spirit, we might be tempted to think that the breath of God was God's Spirit. We might even comfort ourselves with the thought that each and every one of us possesses the Spirit of God within us and that to be human, therefore, is to be divine. Yet, all that God breathed into Adam's nostrils was "breath," what you and I and all others exhale. The gift of the Holy Spirit will remain for God to give on another occasion. We do not possess the gift of the Holy Spirit simply because we are human. Yet, along with all other people in the world, you and I owe our existence to God's breath. The story of Adam helps us recognize that God is the source of our lives.

Beyond that recognition, the story informs us about our identity as human beings. Adam became, the author tells us, "a living being." We could translate the Hebrew words here as "a living soul." In the Hebrew understanding, a soul was the entire person—physical, mental, social. The word, in fact, is often translated as "person," as when we are told in the book of Exodus that "the total number of persons born to Jacob was seventy" (Exodus 1:5). At other times the word is best translated "self" or even "me," as when the psalmist cries to the Lord to "deliver my soul from the sword" (Psalm 22:20).

"A living soul" is who Adam became as a result of the breath of God entering his nostrils and energizing his heart and nourishing his organs. As a soul—that is, a person—Adam needed everything a body requires, and God immediately set out to provide.

A soul needs some place to live, and so God went to work to build in Eden a garden. A soul needs food, and so God planted in that garden trees, some that bore fruit and others that provided ambiance for Adam's dining pleasure. A soul needs something to do with his or her time, something constructive, and so God provided Adam with the occupation of farming the soil, literally, working and protecting it.

A soul needs company, too, and God recognized that on the first day. "It is not good that the man should be alone," God determined. The Lord God, the storyteller informs us, created the animals and paraded them all past Adam to see what he would name them. Not finding among them the partner that Adam needed, God created a woman named Eve.

Now we have two souls running around the garden together. Those two persons enlivened by the breath of God became the basis for human community.

The Bible goes on to discuss the development of many more persons enlivened by the breath of God. They will gather together in places called cities where individuals will contribute their various talents and skills to the welfare of the entire community (Genesis 4:17-22). They will form nations and races, defining community in new and exciting ways (Genesis 10).

Fast Facts
- *Adam* is a Hebrew word that means "humanity."
- *Eve* is a Hebrew word meaning "she gives life."

Whatever form the communities take, they will all bear fitting testimony to the evaluation of God that "it is not good that the man should be alone" (Genesis 2:18). While the breath of God enlivens each and every one of us, our place as "living souls" is together.

EZEKIEL 37:1-14
DRY BONES AND DRY BREATH

Maybe you have been through some of those times that can best be described as "the pits." They are those well-known occasions when nothing seems to have gone right, when you feel all alone, or when you simply feel like giving up on life. If you have, then you have stood in the sandals of the biblical Israelites whose experience at one point in their history led others in a similar situation to sing the old song "Dry Bones."

In 603 B.C., the powerful armies of a Babylonian king named Nebuchadnezzar invaded the city of Jerusalem and carried off some of its leading citizens to their own country. There in Babylon, the people of Jerusalem served as slaves to a previously unknown king. People who had once been court officials, lawyers, doctors, and teachers were now digging canals in a foreign land.

They were in the pits literally. Their pit became even deeper when they learned that 10 years after their deportation, the people back home in Jerusalem revolted against Nebuchadnezzar, and the punishment included the destruction of their beloved city and still another exile of people.

One of the exiles from the first group was a strange man. His name was Ezekiel. He had been trained as a priest, but in Babylon the Lord called him to be a prophet as well. As a prophet he preached God's Word to the people, both prior to the destruction of Jerusalem and afterwards. His message at the beginning was nothing the people wanted to hear. Like many prophets, he preached against the people and their ways and warned them of the impending disaster to befall Jerusalem. When the Babylonians destroyed the city, his sermons changed. He offered hope and even deliverance from the exile in Babylon.

One sermon of hope was couched in a vision. Ezekiel reported that one day the Spirit of the Lord set him down in a valley that was full of bones. They were strewn all over that valley, and had been lying in the hot sun so long that they became very dry.

The prophet himself tells his readers that these bones were the people of Israel. He had listened to their plight often enough to know they had felt downcast and isolated and hopeless. In their own words, their very dry bones meant that "our hope is lost; we are cut off completely" (Ezekiel 37:11).

The bones represented people who were dead, not in the sense of a cessation of brain waves but in the sense of meaninglessness and hopelessness. They were people of a downcast spirit, and that despair dried up their bones. They felt they had no access to God, and that isolation led to the pits.

There in the midst of such despair and hopelessness, the Lord asked Ezekiel if these bones could live again. The prophet could only respond with "God knows!" assuming that God alone did know the answer to the question.

God did know, and so the Lord commanded Ezekiel to prophesy to the bones, those hopeless and despairing people. Ezekiel was to preach the sermon of his life, and it was about life. He was to tell the people that the Lord would "cause breath to enter you, and you shall live" (Ezekiel 37:5).

Ezekiel did as he was told. He preached to the bones about the Lord's breath, and he preached to the breath itself to come from all over the earth and make these bones live. And as he preached, the winds came and brought the breath, and the bones followed the words of the song: they joined together and stood up. They were alive again, thanks to the breath that God sent through his prophet.

Most Bible translations at this point include a footnote indicating that the Hebrew word for "breath" might also be translated

Fast Facts
- Babylon, now what we know as Iraq, was the center of the large and powerful Babylonian Empire that ruled the Middle East from 608 to 539 B.C.
- Nebuchadnezzar was king of Babylon from 605 to 562 B.C.
- The first deportation of people from Jerusalem occurred in 597 B.C. The destruction of the city and the second deportation happened in 587 B.C.

"wind" or "spirit." That information explains why the same Hebrew word is translated "spirit of the Lord" in verse 1, "breath" in most of the story, and "winds" in verse 9. The distinctions appear only in our translations; they are all the same in the original Hebrew.

This word is not the same word as the one in Genesis 2, where God breathed into the nostrils the breath of life. That word means only breath. This word ties up wind and spirit and breath all in one thought, and doing so makes it difficult for us to gain a clear understanding of which is meant.

On the other hand, a little imagination helps us see how these words were considered one thought. In the first place, wind, spirit, and breath are all invisible. We can see the results of their presence but we do not see the wind itself or the spirit or the breath of a person. Second, they involve movement, especially breath and wind—wind stronger than breath unless the breath is God's.

Perhaps to insist on figuring it all out so precisely misses the point. What Ezekiel wanted to accomplish in reporting his vision was to announce that God had not forsaken the people, forlorn and despairing as they were. On the contrary, God was in their midst, stirring up the wind or spirit or breath so that they might rise again, have hope again, live again: "Them bones gonna walk around."

After all, the first time in this vision that Ezekiel uses the word, he says it belongs to the Lord. It was the spirit or wind or breath of God that set the prophet down in the valley. From that point on, the word clearly indicates that the reality that brings life, whether it be spirit or wind or breath, is God's. Like the story in Genesis 2, the message is that God is the source of life. Without God we are dead, literally or figuratively, because life is understood as living in God's presence.

In case any of his readers or hearers missed the message about the breath coming from God to the dry bones, Ezekiel suddenly introduces a new image (verses 12-14). Now the people of Israel are not bones strewn on the ground throughout the valley;

they are buried in graves. The prophet announces clearly the Lord's promise: "I am going to open your graves, and bring you up from your graves, O my people.... I will put my spirit within you, and you shall live...."

Even with the different imagery, the message is the same: the Lord makes alive the dead. The dead in this chapter of Ezekiel are the exiled and hopeless people of Jerusalem. Whether their death-like existence be portrayed as bones on the ground or buried in graves, God's breath or spirit will make them live.

The point is clear: without God there is no life. With God and God's Spirit or breath, the people live. That is Ezekiel's message of good news to the forlorn of his day.

Focus on the Stories

WHO ARE WE?

The stories from Genesis 2 and Ezekiel 37 provide each of us with an identity that is God-given and God-defined. How might these understandings of what it means to be human affect the way we lead our lives from day to day? What does the expression "stewardship of life" mean within this understanding of who we are? How might that identity help us through some difficult times?

REACHING OUT WITH DIGNITY

While the biblical records enable us to know who we are, they simultaneously teach us about the identity and dignity of other people, too. What might such regard for others mean for the way we work with others, meet others in a turnpike tollbooth, treat the person waiting on us in a restaurant? What makes it difficult for us to regard some others with such dignity?

WHY NOT TAKE ALL OF ME?

The author of Genesis 2 challenges us to consider ourselves and others holistically. The story indicates that being defined as "living souls" involves living space, food, occupation, and community. With all this in mind, what might it mean to "love your neighbor as yourself," the commandment Jesus called the second greatest?

How might you, as a member of a congregational community, work toward enabling others to know what God intends for "living souls"?

SPREADING THE WORD OF LIFE
The story from Ezekiel indicates that without God and God's Spirit, people are considered the walking dead. Think of some persons whose lives are in the pits at the moment and who cannot find any reason for hope. Perhaps someone who is grieving the death of a loved one comes to mind. How might you bring the Spirit of God to that person so that he or she might find life again?

For the Next Session
Since the breath of God gives life here and now, God promises to send his Spirit to inspire life in the kingdom to come.

Closing

You show me the path of life.
In your presence there is fullness of joy;
in your right hand are pleasures forevermore.

—Psalm 16:11

The Spirit of God's Future Reign

To a world entrapped in
hopelessness, God promises to
send the Spirit as part of God's reign.

ISAIAH 11:1-10
GOD'S PROMISED SPIRIT FOR THE KING

The people of biblical Israel had as much trouble with their kings as we today have with politicians. Their experiences with royalty left much to be desired.

For several centuries after Solomon (king of Israel and Judah) died, the people had two kings on two different thrones. Israel was the name of the kingdom in the north, one with its own king—elected or replaced after timely assassinations. Political life in Israel was chaotic. Its instability caused problems for the people—so much trouble that the king or the crown itself did not play a vital role in their life and faith.

In the south, however, the kingdom of Judah was totally dependent upon the crown. The reigning king was regarded as the sign of stability for the people. Whether or not he proved efficient or faithful or benign, the king represented the power and authority of the Lord.

Why was that? Back in the days of King David, the Lord made a promise that there would always sit on Jerusalem's throne one of the descendants of David. Actually, it was more than a descendant. It was the first son of the preceding king. In other words, God established a dynasty with David and promised that succession would occur the way the world has come to expect of dynasties.

God established the dynasty of David so that God could exercise rule over the people through this particular form of government. The dynasty was the way that God would see that justice was done, that the poor would be cared for, that the vulnerable in the society would be protected. Some of the psalms, like Psalm 72, indicated to the king his responsibilities on behalf of God.

Unfortunately the hand of God was difficult to discern in the ways kings ruled. Power often corrupted the kings. As a result, the people of Judah longed for an ideal king. They hoped that God would provide such a king so that God's rule might be evident in their lives.

The prophet Isaiah knew well what was expected of a godly king of davidic descent. The "handwriting" was on the wall and so were Assryian troops. The destruction of Jerusalem was about to happen.

Isaiah's faith in the Lord's promise to rule the people through such a king remained strong, even in the midst of the coming disaster. He announced that the Assyrians would destroy the city. Whether or not they realized it, the Assyrians were the instruments of God in bringing judgment on the city for its unfaithfulness to God. Yet God would be faithful to the promise.

Fast Facts

◆ David was king over Judah and Israel from 1000 until 961 B.C.
◆ Solomon, David's son and successor, ruled over Judah and Israel from 961 until 922 B.C.
◆ Jerusalem means "the city of peace."

The prophet delivered his vision of the coming days (Isaiah 10:33—11:10). The Lord would bring devastation on the city the way a forester goes through the woods, lopping the boughs, felling the trees, hacking the thickets. Life for Jerusalem and its crown seemed hopeless.

But, the prophet announced, out of one of those stumps, the one that belonged to the family of Jesse (David's father) a little sprig would reach for the sun. That image described the new descendant of David who would emerge as the promised king.

This ruler would do everything right. He would exercise justice throughout the land with divinely-inspired insight. The poor and the meek would receive the justice God required for them. The ruthless and the wicked would know the Lord's wrath.

Under his reign everything would seem like paradise. Animals that presently devour one another would live together and dine side by side. Even young children will play in the vicinity of poisonous snakes without the slightest harm.

What will make this king different from all those who preceded him? God will bestow on this king God's Spirit. This Spirit is:

"the spirit of wisdom and understanding,
the spirit of counsel and might,
the spirit of knowledge and the fear of the Lord."

—Isaiah 11:2

All these words describe a very wise and faithful person. "The fear of the Lord is the beginning of knowledge," announces the old saying (Proverbs 1:7). And in that fundamental response of "fear of the Lord," that is, complete obedience and awe of God, this ideal king will delight.

The gift of God's Spirit will enable this king to be like no other. Endowed with that divine Spirit, the davidic king will possess the faithfulness and wisdom and insight to rule in such a way that all the people will know peace. Even the animals in his kingdom will live in harmony. The scene is called appropriately "the peaceable kingdom," and it is the result of the Spirit of God directing the life and work of the king to come.

Isaiah and the people of his time never experienced that king. The people of Judaism still wait for his coming, for the one promised here is none other than the Lord's Messiah.

Christians believe that the expected Messiah has indeed come, endowed with the Spirit of God. The ministry, death, and resurrection of Jesus of Nazareth, son of David and son of God, was the beginning of that kingdom. Until Jesus comes again, we wait, too, for the peaceable kingdom.

JOEL 2:28-29
GOD'S PROMISE OF THE SPIRIT ON ALL

Life does seem topsy-turvy sometimes. The daily news in the newspapers or on television makes us wonder where the world is headed. Children march into schools with firearms to kill their classmates and teachers. Relations among races are strained to the point of violence. Abuse within families threatens the health and well-being of millions.

Where is the world headed? The question is not a modern invention. Almost twenty-five hundred years ago, the people of Israel were asking the same question. They had just experienced a series of disasters, not the least of which was a plague of locusts that devoured their crops. Their whole economy felt the effects. People had no money to buy food for their families.

Of course, when times go bad like that, somebody must be blamed. All kinds of irrational behavior take over. Adversity does not always bring people together. They get angry more easily than in normal times. They are less patient. They cannot find hope.

Into that situation came the prophet Joel. His preaching announced that the situation could be worse before it improves. God, however, was offering them the opportunity to return to him with their whole heart. At the same time, God was promising them an abundant crop and times for rejoicing. Then came the big news.

The Lord would bring about a new world. God would turn all their sorrow into joy, all their poverty into prosperity, all their famine into abundance. Best of all, the Lord would send his Spirit among them on the coming day. God would pour out the Spirit with such generosity that everybody would be covered from head to toe (Joel 2:28-29).

Everybody included sons and daughters, young and old, male and female slaves. All the separations that the society of the day had manufactured would be washed away by God's outpouring of the Spirit. No group of people could say it had a corner on the spirit market. No group could exclude another as being unworthy of the Spirit. No one could pull rank over another. They would all have the same gift of the Spirit, and that gift would make them one in the midst of their divisions and their fragmentation.

Joel was not the first prophet to look toward the day of God's reign. Neither was he the first to recognize that on that day, God would welcome the people who had been left out, literally cast out, of the religious establishment.

Three hundred years before Joel, the prophet Micah announced that God's reign would include the lame, the afflicted, and the castoffs (Micah 4:6-7). That in itself was a sermon to turn the world upside down, because in that society, those who were afflicted in some way were considered to be under the curse of God and therefore excluded from the "decent folks." God had other plans in store, Micah declared. They would become clear when God began to reign over the world.

A contemporary of Micah's, the prophet Isaiah, also looked to the new day as a time of rejoicing—instead of the present distress. He announced to the people that in the kingdom to come, the deaf would hear, the lame would leap, and those unable to speak would sing for joy (Isaiah 35). Isaiah looked to a time when the world would be turned upside down.

Among all the prophets prior to Joel who delivered God's promise of a new day to come, only Ezekiel spoke of the gift of God's Spirit as one of the signs of that new day. One of those occasions was in his vision of the dry bones (Ezekiel 37:1-4). He spoke of God's Spirit as the means by which the people of Israel would be able to keep God's commandments (36:26-27). Yet Ezekiel spoke of the outpouring of God's Spirit only on the people of Israel.

It appears that Joel saw a bigger picture. He envisioned the new day when God would pour out his Spirit "on all flesh" (Joel 2:28). He envisioned the new day of God's reign as the time when all people would receive the gift of God's Spirit, causing women as well as men to prophesy.

According to Joel's vision, prophecy is the result of God's Spirit. What is prophecy? We often think it means predicting future events. Sometimes it does, especially when the future is the new day when God's reign breaks into human history. Prophets sometimes spoke of impending disaster, especially when the danger of invading armies loomed large on their horizon.

Basically, however, prophecy means "speaking on behalf of someone else." That someone else was, for the biblical prophets, none other than the Lord God. God spoke the word of comfort to people when they were afflicted. God spoke the word of judgment when the people were all too comfortable. The prophet Ezekiel attributed his ability to prophesy to the Spirit of God. Joel envisioned that the outpouring of God's Spirit would enable all people, men and women alike, to speak on God's behalf.

According to Joel's prophecy, God's gift of the Spirit would also enable young and old to dream dreams and see visions. Far from fantasy, hallucination, or illusion, dreams and visions are the means by which prophets could see beyond the brokenness of everyday life to the splendor of God's reign. It was a vision that Isaiah announced when he spoke of all nations flowing to Jerusalem in order to worship and praise the Lord, a time when all people would lay down their weapons (Isaiah 2:2-4). It was a vision that enabled Ezekiel to announce new life to the dry bones in the valley (Ezekiel 37). It was a vision that Joel announced when he spoke of the outpouring of God's Spirit.

Fast Facts
- Isaiah and Micah were prophets in the latter half of the eighth century B.C.
- Joel was a prophet in the fourth century B.C.
- *Messiah* is a Hebrew word that means "the anointed one."

A vision is what faith is about. It casts our minds and hearts beyond the horizon to recognize the reality of God's promises. "Now faith is the assurance of things hoped for, the conviction of things not seen" (Hebrews 11:1).

Joel offered his listeners a vision on which they could hang their hearts and hopes. Trapped as they were in the famine and poverty resulting from the locust attack, the people needed a vision of hope.

Distorted as they were in their views about one another, especially about different races and nations, the people needed to glimpse a vision of the oneness of humanity in the blessing of the Spirit.

As one of God's visionaries, a prophet of the Lord, Joel knew what they needed. They needed God's Spirit. We too pray that it would come to turn the world upside down!

Focus on the Stories

LIVING WITH GOD'S PROMISE

The promise of the peaceable kingdom continues, even though Jesus Christ has come as the expected Messiah. How does it feel to keep waiting? What difference does it make in your life to know that the Spirit-endowed Messiah has already come?

GOVERNMENT'S ROLE

Read Psalm 72 and Paul's Letter to the Romans 13:1-7 as you reflect on the following question. Does the role given to the davidic kings of Judah play any part in what we should expect of our governments, particularly in regard to the poor?

IMAGINING OPPOSITES

On a sheet of chart paper or the chalkboard, write down some of the items of bad news that have been reported in the past month. Include as well some bad news experiences that are closer to you and your family. What would be the opposite of all those experiences? Write them down in a column opposite the bad news items. How does the visioning discussed here provide hope in such times?

BESTOWING THE SPIRIT

Immediately after a person is baptized, the pastor prays for the Spirit to be with and within that individual. In the prayer in the order for Holy Baptism in *Lutheran Book of Worship*, the Holy

Spirit is described as "the spirit of wisdom and understanding, the spirit of counsel and might, the spirit of knowledge and the fear of the Lord, the spirit of joy in your presence." What do these words mean to you in light of the discussion about the Spirit that is promised for the Messiah to come (Isaiah 11)?

REMOVING THE BARRIERS
The attitudes some people bear against others often fragment the world in which we live. Notions of superiority and inferiority, power and vulnerability often result simply because we are different, have different roles in life, or reside in different neighborhoods. How does the vision of God's Spirit poured out on everyone challenge those attitudes?

For the Next Session
God fulfills the promised gift of the Spirit following Jesus' resurrection.

Closing
… We must concentrate on the term "Holy Spirit," because it is so precise that we can find no substitute for it. Many other kinds of spirits are mentioned in the Scriptures, such as the spirit of man, heavenly spirits, and the evil spirit. But God's Spirit alone is called the Holy Spirit….

—Martin Luther

The Book of Concord, tr./ed. Theodore G. Tappert (Philadelphia: Fortress Press, 1959)

A New Breath of Life

*God sends the Holy Spirit, as
promised, to give new life by creating
the church and sending it into the world.*

ACTS 2:1-21
THE FIRE THAT FEEDS US

Imagine showing up for worship as usual when something happens to change the world! That is precisely what happened 50 days after Jesus rose from the dead.

The disciples and tens of thousands of Jewish people from all over the world gathered in Jerusalem for the annual festival of Pentecost. It was one of three festivals in the year when Jews were to gather at the temple in Jerusalem. Called the Feast of Weeks in the Old Testament, the festival was held 50 days after Passover. It marked the beginning of the first fruits harvest offering to God whose blessing provided the grain. In the midst of the assembly, the disciples of Jesus huddled together.

Suddenly a loud noise sounding like winds of hurricane force startled everyone. Then came a strangeness that is impossible to imagine. "Tongues as of fire" danced around in their midst until one hovered over the head of each disciple.

However we picture the event, what matters is what it means. In the Old Testament, wind and fire are often signs of the presence of God. Since no one could actually see God, people could realize God's presence by such signs as thunder, earthquake, wind, and fire. Even the burning bush that Moses experienced

(Exodus 3:1-6) was a sign that God was at hand with power and mystery.

Now comes the moment for which we have been waiting! The Holy Spirit, signified by tongues of flame, came upon the disciples, and they began to speak fluently in languages they had never known. This spectacular communication was possible because "the Spirit gave them ability" (Acts 2:4).

What made all this activity especially surprising was that the other people gathered there, people from all over the Mediterranean world, people who spoke a variety of languages, each heard these disciples speaking "about God's deeds of power" in their own languages! They wondered aloud at the simple folk from Galilee who spoke like polished professional interpreters.

We would expect that most of the people observing this strange phenomenon would wonder aloud, "What's going on here?" And we would expect that some would be ready with a quick, if cynical, answer. "They are filled with new wine," they said with a sneer (Acts 2:13).

The disciple Peter, often the spokesperson for the others, took on his preacher's voice and boomed out over the crowd, "Indeed, these are not drunk, as you suppose, for it is only nine o'clock in the morning" (Acts 2:15). Peter then begins to explain what this means.

Peter told them that this miracle of languages is due to the fulfillment of God's promise to send his Spirit, the prophecy from the second chapter of Joel. This event meant that the new day of God's reign that the prophet Joel had announced, had arrived. The proof was in this audiovisual demonstration of the Holy Spirit's power. Just as the prophet Joel announced, the Holy Spirit created a miracle of prophecy to mark the beginning of God's everlasting rule on earth.

Fast Facts

- *Pentecost* means "the 50th day."
- Peter was the chief spokesperson for the 12 disciples.
- Judas Iscariot means Judas, "the man from Kerioth," a village of unknown location.
- Mount Sinai is a mountain located according to tradition in the southern part of the Sinai Peninsula between Egypt and Saudi Arabia.

Peter quoted more from Joel's prophecy. Blood and fire and smoky mist would appear "before the coming of the Lord's great and glorious day" (Acts 2:20). That list of natural phenomena fits well with the appearance of God on Mount Sinai in the days of Moses (Exodus 19:16-19). It also sounds like the description of the Lord's coming on the last day: "For the Lord will come in fire, and his chariots like the whirlwind, to pay back his anger in fury, and his rebuke in flames of fire" (Isaiah 66:15).

In case anyone in that crowd gathered for Pentecost missed the meaning of the fire, Peter explained it clearly. God was present in their midst.

Unlike the prophecy, however, this gift of the Holy Spirit in the Lord's new day did not result in devastation. The focus of this event was on the gift of the Holy Spirit that people might prophesy. Through their prophesying, others would hear the Word of God and come to faith. This was God's purpose: "everyone who calls on the name of the Lord shall be saved" (Acts 2:21 from Joel 2:32).

Because of the gift of the Holy Spirit, the early church gave new meaning to the festival of Pentecost. Among Christians the festival would no longer celebrate the agricultural harvest event with the fruits of the earth, but a spiritual harvest abounding in the fruits of the Spirit. To this day, the festival marks the gift of the Holy Spirit and is celebrated as the birthday of the Christian church.

We celebrate Pentecost 50 days after after the day of resurrection. We change the color in our churches from the white of the Easter season to red, the color of fire, the sign of the Holy Spirit.

Pentecost celebrates the gift of the Holy Spirit so that people might be able to speak "about God's deeds of power" (Acts 2:11). Pentecost is first and foremost about the everyday witnessing to the power of God at work in human lives, the same power that raised Jesus from the dead. The Holy Spirit empowered ordinary men and women to proclaim a message powerful enough to transform lives, to change the course of history. These spirited disciples little resembled the horrified, helpless selves they had been on Good Friday, the day Jesus died.

JOHN 20:19-23
FRESH AIR FOR A GASPING WORLD

The writer of the Gospel of John tells of the coming of the Holy Spirit differently than the writer of Acts. Both however, remind us of Christ's promise to always be with us. Still, the disciples in John's Gospel didn't know that yet; just imagine what the disciples must have felt when Jesus was crucified. The teacher they had been following for three years had been arrested and executed Roman-style: nailed to a cross. They had obviously placed high hopes in Jesus, but then those hopes had been hammered to death.

Very early on the Sunday morning after Jesus' death and burial, Mary Magdalene discovered that the tomb was empty. Shocked, she ran to get Simon Peter and the disciple Jesus loved, and showed them the cave's emptiness. Not knowing what to make of it, the two men returned home while Mary lingered at the tomb. Suddenly two angels appeared to her, and while she was busy sorting out her questions, Jesus stood beside her. She turned and glanced at him through her tears, but didn't recognize him. Then he called her by name and she knew. As he instructed, she ran back to the disciples saying, "I have seen the Lord" (John 20:18). The author of John's Gospel gives no indication that the disciples believed a word of it.

That same evening, however, Mary's message was confirmed! Afraid for their own lives because of what the Jewish religious leaders did to Jesus, the disciples locked themselves in some room in the city of Jerusalem. Suddenly Jesus was in their midst, despite the locked door. He greeted them with the reassuring words, "Peace be with you" (John 20:19). He showed them the marks from the nails in his hands and the hole in his side from the soldier's spear. Jesus proved he was the same person they last saw gasping for breath on a cross. The disciples now knew they were not seeing an apparition. This person was the crucified one, yet alive in every way.

As the resurrected one, Jesus wasted no time in announcing his purpose. "As the Father has sent me, so I send you" (John 20:21). Perhaps they wondered where he was sending them, or perhaps they remembered that they had heard those words before. The evening he was arrested, Jesus had prayed for them out loud. They heard Jesus tell God, "As you have sent me into the world, so I have sent them into the world" (17:18).

Now, behind the locked doors, when Jesus said he was sending them, they knew what that meant. They would face the world the way Jesus did, and be misunderstood as he was. The world, Jesus had already informed them, would reject them just as surely as it rejected the Father and the Son. The world, according to the Gospel of John, stood against God and everything the reign of God was promised to be.

Yet it was into the world that the resurrected Jesus was sending them. That sending is the meaning of mission: God's reaching out to the broken world through people chosen for the task. The prospects of such a mission might scare any disciple into fleeing the responsibility. The first disciples might have done just that—— except for one reason: Jesus gave them the Holy Spirit.

"When he had said this, he breathed on them and said to them, 'Receive the Holy Spirit. If you forgive the sins of any, they are forgiven them; if you retain the sins of any, they are retained'" (John 20:22-23).

There is that breath again! God breathed into the nostrils of the clay mannequin the breath of life, and Adam came alive. God breathed through the preaching of the prophet Ezekiel into the despairing people of Jerusalem exiled in

Fast Facts

◆ Mary Magdalene is so named because of her hometown in Magdala, a tiny place on the shore of the Sea of Galilee.

◆ Galilee is the northern section of Israel where almost all of Jesus' ministry occurred.

◆ *Mission*, meaning "sending," has been the work of God ever since the time of Abraham and Sarah; the purpose of God's mission has always been to bring blessing.

Babylon, and they were able to live again in hope. Now Jesus, resurrected from the dead, breathes on the disciples and identifies his breath as the Holy Spirit. This Spirit will enable the disciples to perform the work of God, breathing life into a dying world.

Although different from the Day of Pentecost reported in Acts 2, this story represents John's stylized version of the birthday of the church. This author of this Gospel combines the resurrection, Jesus' ascension to the Father, and the gift of the Holy Spirit all into one grand Easter event. In both versions, the gift of the Spirit comes as a result of Jesus' resurrection, and sends the disciples to the peoples of the world with power and grace.

The Spirit gives the church the authority to forgive or to retain sins. Forgiving sin had been God's purpose all along. In the Old Testament God provided various means for the forgiveness of the sins of the people Israel. Sin is the name for the human rebellion that set a barrier between God and the people. Forgiveness is the name for God's removal of that barrier so that God's life and grace can flow to the people God dearly loves. In ancient times, God established a system of sacrifices so that forgiveness could be granted through specific means of worship (see Exodus 29:38-46). God invited confession through prayer so that forgiveness might be granted, as so many of the psalms demonstrate (see Psalm 32:5). God encouraged the people of Israel to turn to him (repent) and live, because God did not desire the death of anyone (Ezekiel 18:32).

Now God extends the gift of divine forgiveness to the world, and the means to accomplish that purpose is the Spirit-endowed church. The thought is staggering! The world that rejects God and Jesus and the church is the target audience for the message about God's gift of forgiveness.

In spite of itself, the world is the object of God's love. "For God so loved the world that he gave his only Son, so that everyone who believes in him may not perish but may have eternal life" (John 3:16). The only way the world can know that unconditional, surprising love of God is through the church's announcement of the death and resurrection of Jesus Christ.

As for retaining sins (the other side of Jesus' commission), that responsibility is not an active one but a passive one. The church, inspired by the Holy Spirit, announces God's gifts through Jesus Christ. As long as the world continues its hostility to the Father and to the Son and to the Holy Spirit, the world retains its own sin. It denies the gift of forgiveness, and it maintains the barrier God offers to break down. The gift is free and unconditional, but even that gift can be rejected, especially when it flies in the face of the way the world goes about its business. The world is bent not on forgiveness but on vengeance, not on love but hatred, not on compassion but on violence. The first 10 minutes of your local news broadcast prove the point.

As hostile as the world is, nevertheless it is still the world that God loves. It is the world to which God sends the church. It is in the world that the Holy Spirit inspires the church to perform its ministry of forgiving sins.

If we are honest about our feelings regarding the church and world, we might admit it would be easier to remain, as the disciples attempted, behind closed doors. Venturing forth into the chaotic world involves risks and challenges. Yet the risen Christ did not commend the disciples for their attempted security. He sent them with the Holy Spirit into a world gasping for breath.

Focus on the Stories

TIME ZONES

The gift of the Holy Spirit marks the fulfillment of God's promise. That gift means the expected reign of God has begun, in short, a new time. Apart from changing the reckoning of time from B.C. (before Christ) to A.D. (*anno Domini*, "the year of the Lord"), what difference does it make to you to live in this new time? Does it affect the way you think? The way you behave?

PROPHETS ONE AND ALL

The Day of Pentecost announces that the whole church is endowed with the Holy Spirit in order to prophesy and see visions. Does the role of prophet or visionary sound appealing to you? How do you prophesy (speak on behalf of God) in your daily life and work? Do you look beyond everyday experiences to envision the promises of God for life and hope? If and when you do, are you aware that the Holy Spirit is lifting your eyes to a faith-filled reality?

FACING THE WORLD

Whether the Holy Spirit is inspiring us to speak about "God's deeds of power" (Acts 2:11) or to forgive and retain sins (John 20:23), God is clear about the role of the church: to be involved in the world. Is this the way you have thought about the church? What are the risks both to yourself and to the church of getting heavily involved in the world? Consider some of the difficulties. What are the alternatives? Are they appropriate alternatives for a Spirit-endowed church?

THE MEANING OF SPIRITUALITY

Many people talk about the need for a more spiritual approach to life. What do you think is meant by the word *spirituality*? If you have read or listened to those who focus on spirituality, what are they suggesting? As you consider the two Bible passages in this session, how do you believe *spirituality* is defined? Is it the same as or different than the way people generally use the word?

For the Next Session

How do we come to believe that God was in Christ, and how does that faith change our lives?

Closing

Widen our love, good Spirit, to embrace
In your strong care all those of every race.
Like wind and fire with life among us move,
Till we are known as Christ's, and Christians prove.

—John R. Peacey (*Lutheran Book of Worship* #160)

God's Truth

Through the Holy Spirit, God
opens our eyes to the truth and
calls the church to witness in the world.

JOHN 16:12-15
THE SPIRIT OF TRUTH

The time was growing short. Jesus had so much to teach his disciples before he would die. There was no question about what was coming. Jesus' message and miracles had made him a threat to the religious leaders. They were determined to find a way to rid the world of him.

Jesus knew the difficulty his disciples would have facing all the events about to take place. They had trouble enough understanding what his teachings meant even when he was around to explain them. Soon, Jesus realized, they would have to absorb both the meaning of his death and the awesome surprise of his resurrection. How would they grasp all that?

Gathered in a room somewhere in Jerusalem, Jesus tried to prepare the disciples for his death. Judas, who had already agreed to betray Jesus, left the room and fled into the night. With Judas gone, Jesus taught the remaining disciples all that he could cram into one after-dinner discussion. He told them several times that his command was that they love one another with the same kind of love he would show them by dying for them on a cross. He promised to prepare a place for them in his Father's house so that they would all come together again.

Until that heavenly reunion, Jesus promised, he would care for them in a number of ways. Above all, he promised them the Holy Spirit. Jesus called the Spirit "the Advocate," that is, one who would stand at their side to plead their cause. He also called the Holy Spirit "the Spirit of truth," and he promised it would be present in and among them (John 14:16-17).

What would this Holy Spirit do for them and the rest of the church? In the first place, the Spirit "will teach you everything, and remind you of all that I have said to you" (John 14:26). Surely, over the course of those three years, Jesus had said many things that were vital to their understanding of who he was and what God was doing in his ministry. The Spirit would help them remember and respond.

Here is an example. Three years earlier, the first time he had brought the disciples with him to Jerusalem, Jesus drove out the money changers from the temple. Forced by the startled Jewish audience to explain why and by what authority he did this, Jesus said, "Destroy this temple, and in three days I will raise it up" (John 2:19). After the author of the Fourth Gospel explained for his readers that Jesus was speaking of his own body, he added, "After he was raised from the dead, his disciples remembered that he had said this; and they believed the scripture and the word that Jesus had spoken" (John 2:22). Only after Easter Day—the same day that Jesus breathed on them and said, "Receive the Holy Spirit!"—could the disciples remember that saying and comprehend what it meant for faith. The first thing the Holy Spirit accomplished was to establish Jesus' identity to his disciples.

What else would the Spirit do? Jesus said, "When the Advocate comes, whom I will send to you from the Father, the Spirit of truth who comes from the Father, he will testify on my behalf" (John 15:26). Like a character witness in a court case, the Holy Spirit would verify who Jesus was: the only Son of the Father. Without that testimony in the world, who could possibly come to believe the fact that this carpenter from Nazareth, the one who was executed in the manner of a common criminal, was the Son of God?

Convincing the world that rejected him of his true identity was the work of the Holy Spirit. Yet how did that work get accomplished? The following verse seems to point directly to the answer. "You also are to testify because you have been with me from the beginning" (John 15:27). The testimony of the Holy Spirit about Jesus was the same as the testimony of the disciples about Jesus. They had heard his words and had seen his works; the Holy Spirit enabled them to remember his words and works in order to tell others about him. All this testimony came together as one and the same: the Holy Spirit's testimony about Jesus took place in the quiet inspiration of the disciples, while the disciples' inspired testimony about Jesus occurred in the words they spoke and the deeds they did.

The third function of the Holy Spirit was to convict the world of its sin (John 16:8-11). Throughout this difficult evening with the disciples, Jesus had been telling them that the world had rejected him, and the proof of that hostility would occur in a matter of hours. By rejecting him, Jesus said, the world rejected the Father, because it was the Father who sent him. Now Jesus sends the disciples into that same world. It will reject them as surely as it rejected him and the Father. This rejection of God, Jesus, and the disciples is the world's sin. The Holy Spirit would prove the world wrong in all this rebellion.

Finally, the task of the Holy Spirit was to take Jesus' words and declare them to the disciples (John 16:12-15). In this way the ministry of Jesus could continue in the world. The Spirit of truth guaranteed that from generation to generation the ministry of Jesus and

Fast Facts

♦ While Jesus spoke on several occasions about "his Father's house" as the temple in Jerusalem, he meant here the kingdom of God where the Father reigns.

♦ The temple in Jerusalem was expanded and remodeled by Herod the Great about 20 B.C. and destroyed by the Romans in A.D. 70.

♦ The words *testify* and *witness* are often used interchangeably.

the announcement about Jesus would continue throughout the world, even the world that rejects him and the message.

ROMANS 12:1-2
THE GOSPEL IN THE FLESH

The author of this letter to the Romans is the apostle Paul. His parents knew him as Saul. The biblical story of his transformation from Saul to Paul involves much more than his name.

We meet Saul in Acts 7:58 where he is introduced as a man who approvingly stood by while a disciple of the resurrected Jesus was being stoned to death. The executed man was Stephen, a man full of faith and the Holy Spirit, who was chosen along with six others to witness to the Lord. Upon hearing Stephen's preaching, Saul became enraged at his message and at all Christians. He dedicated himself to finding Christians in the city of Jerusalem and dragging them off to prison. Not content with ridding Jerusalem of the followers of Jesus, Saul asked permission to go to the city of Damascus and do the same favor for the people there.

Permission granted, Saul journeyed toward Damascus. On the way, the risen Christ appeared to him on the road, changing him so dramatically that he soon became a disciple of Jesus himself, preaching and teaching in the synagogues that the Jesus who was crucified and raised was the Messiah, God's anointed ruler. The whole story appears first in Acts 9. It is repeated in Acts 26 and Galatians 1. The repetition shows clearly how important this conversion of Saul was for the church and for the future of Christianity.

In time Saul, too, was filled with the Holy Spirit. Like Jesus sending out the apostles with the gift of the Spirit, the Holy Spirit sent Saul to all parts of the Roman Empire where the message was to be preached. Saul began to be known also as Paul (Acts 13:9).

The apostle Paul traveled all over the areas we know today as Turkey, Greece, and even Italy. His preaching brought people to faith, and as a result, congregations were formed in many communities. Paul continued his contact with them through repeated visits. He also dealt with a variety of matters by sending them letters which now comprise about one quarter of the New Testament.

The longest letter is the one known as the Epistle to the Romans. Written around A.D. 55 or 56, the letter addressed a congregation that consisted of Christians from Jewish and from Gentile backgrounds. Paul suggested at one point in this letter that the mere fact that Jews and Gentiles worship the Lord together is proof that the reign of God has begun. It was one of the miracles expected for the day when God would establish the kingdom.

That inclusiveness of the Christian community was an essential part of his letter. In the first two chapters, Paul demonstrated that all people, Jews and Gentiles, are guilty of the sin that separates us from God. His point is that, while all are guilty of sin, all are also given the gift of the gospel. He described that gift primarily with the word *justification*. The word, borrowed from the legal courts of the day, basically meant acquittal. Having demonstrated that all are guilty, the surprise occurs when the judge announces that all are forgiven and can go free. "For there is no distinction, since all have sinned and fall short of the glory of God; they are now justified by his grace as a gift..." (Romans 3:22-23).

The eight chapters that follow spell out in various ways the meaning of this gift for "all." Paul concludes this long section with an eloquent Wow!—"O the depth of the riches and wisdom and knowledge of God! How unsearchable are his judgments and how inscrutable his ways!" (Romans 11:33). That the guilty should be declared innocent and set free is an awesome bit of news.

Fast Facts

◆ The book of Acts is the second volume of a larger work of which the first volume is the Gospel According to Luke.

◆ Stephen is remembered by the church as the first Christian martyr. A martyr is someone who dies for his or her beliefs.

◆ Gentile refers generally to someone who is not Jewish. In the Old Testament such people are called "the nations."

◆ Damascus is a city in Syria, about 135 miles from Jerusalem.

◆ *Apostle* means "one who is sent out."

That news is the basis for the beginning of the next section of the letter. It is what comes before the word *therefore* in our Bible passage. "I appeal to you therefore, brothers and sisters, by the mercies of God, to present your bodies as a living sacrifice, holy and acceptable to God, which is your spiritual worship" (Romans 12:1). God's sacrifice of Jesus Christ for our justification is the basis of the appeal that Christians offer their bodies as a living sacrifice.

Such sacrificial offering of our bodies is our "spiritual worship." Paul defines *spiritual* in physical terms, our bodily involvement in the world as a giving of oneself to serve the world, just as Jesus did. Far from a private exercise in which we shoot our minds heavenward, spirituality for a Christian means active public participation in the world for Jesus' sake, employing every skill of heart and spirit, mind and strength. This involvement is "holy and acceptable to God," that is, fitting for those who have received God's wondrous gift of justification and honor God by the way we live our lives.

In the cultures of Paul's day, sacrifices were familiar. Sometimes the sacrifices consisted of grain and other agricultural products; sometimes an animal; in some cases a human child or adult. An elaborate system of sacrifices, agricultural and animal (never human) appears in the Old Testament as one way God extended forgiveness to ancient Israel.

What the apostle Paul appeals for here, however, is not the death of a person. Paul appeals to Christians to offer their bodies "as a living sacrifice." Living, not dying, is the point here: living our physical lives as a demonstration of the spiritual gift of justification.

Approaching the world and life itself from that perspective of spirituality requires a new way of thinking. "Do not be conformed to this world, but be transformed by the renewing of your minds, so that you may discern what is the will of God—what is good and acceptable and perfect" (Romans 12:2). Footnotes in most Bibles indicate that the word translated as "world" is the Greek word for "age" or "era." The message is clear: now that the new day of God's reign has begun, people of faith must learn to think and function in a new way.

Most of the world still lives as though nothing significant happened with Jesus. They go about their self-centered ways bent on violence, greed, and vengeance. That is the thinking of an age that is ending. Those who are justified by God are called to discern God's will and live life ahead of their time, in God's new age.

The coming of the Holy Spirit established a new time zone. Christians, God's kingdom people, are called to think, act, and feel differently, to live in honor of God—that is, in service to the world God loves.

Focus on the Stories

UNCOMPREHENDING DISCIPLES

During Jesus' ministry on earth, the disciples had a difficult time understanding what he was all about, who he really was, and what could be accomplished by his death. How do you respond to the disciples' inability to grasp the truth? Does it frighten you that the disciples were the ones in whom Jesus entrusted the gospel? Is it comforting to realize that the disciples, too, had difficulty getting it all together?

OUR ADVOCATE

We often hear people begin an argument by saying, "I'm going to play the devil's advocate." What do they mean by that statement? What would it mean to take the devil's side in an argument? In John's Gospel, Jesus called the Holy Spirit "the Advocate." He implied a particular function the Spirit of God would serve for God and for the church. How does that title for the Holy Spirit help or not help your understanding of who the Spirit is and what the Spirit does for the church?

IT'S UNBELIEVABLE!

In his explanation to the Third Article of the Apostles' Creed, Martin Luther began by admitting, "I believe that by my own understanding or strength I cannot believe in Jesus Christ my Lord or come to him" (*A Contemporary Translation of Luther's Small Catechism: Study Edition*, tr./ed. Timothy J. Wengert [Mpls: Augsburg Fortress, 1994]).

Is that true for you as well? Is the message about Jesus, who he is and what God accomplished through him, at all comprehensible through our mental and physical efforts? Luther continues to explain how he does come to believe this otherwise unbelievable message. "But instead the Holy Spirit has called me through the Gospel, enlightened me with his gifts, made me holy and kept me in the true faith..." (*A Contemporary Translation of Luther's Small Catechism: Study Edition*). Does this statement connect at all to the teachings of Jesus in Bible passages we studied in this session? Does it make sense in your own experience in coming to believe in Jesus Christ? Where do doubts fit into this approach?

WORLDLY SPIRITUALITY

If spirituality is the offering of our bodies as living sacrifices in the world, what does that mean for the way you live your life day in and day out? Beyond yourself as an individual, what does such an understanding of spirituality say about the way your congregation goes about its ministry? Why do you think people tend to define *spirituality* in an otherworldly way?

For the Next Session

If the Holy Spirit works not only in us but among us, what does that say about our lives together as a church?

Closing

Lord God, you taught the hearts of your faithful people by sending them the light of your Holy Spirit. Grant that we, by your Spirit, may have a right judgment in all things and evermore rejoice in his holy counsel; through your Son, Jesus Christ our Lord.

—Prayer for Enlightenment of the Holy Spirit
(*Lutheran Book of Worship*, p. 47)

The Web of Community

*Against our human
attempts to go our separate ways,
the Holy Spirit brings us into a new
community called the church.*

1 CORINTHIANS 12:1-13
ONE SPIRIT, ONE COMMUNITY

The word *spiritual* was as common in the days of Paul the
apostle as it is today. Today the term can mean just about any-
thing. People use the word to mean everything from soaking themselves in nature to listening to music to running a marathon.
Living a spiritual life for some means Bible reading and prayer;
others find spiritual expression in the way they arrange the furni-
ture (Feng Shui). The first century Christians in Corinth also held
wide-ranging opinions about what spiritual living meant.

The apostle Paul took up the discussion in his lively corre-
spondence with the Christians in Corinth. Two letters (epistles) in
the New Testament are addressed to that community.

Corinth was an important Greek city located on a gulf by
the same name. Many travelers passed through Corinth. Along
with the variety of people came many ideas, philosophies, and
religions.

After Paul preached the gospel of Jesus Christ to the
Corinthians, a congregation formed. The members struggled with
this new faith concerning Jesus' death and resurrection. Some
wondered about its connections with Judaism, its laws and

customs. Others tried to understand what this faith meant in comparison with some of the religions, philosophies, and practices they had known from their Greek world.

From that ancient culture, people were well acquainted with the "spiritual gifts" expressed by some people. Indeed, not far from Corinth, high in the mountains overlooking the gulf, was the city of Delphi where for many centuries, people came from far and wide to consult the spirit-endowed women who uttered oracles. Such people were held in high esteem, considered to be favored by the gods.

What challenged the apostle Paul in that setting was not the question of the existence of spiritual powers. That was assumed. The questions were "Which spirit?" and "For what purpose?"

The Spirit that Paul spoke about was not one that caused selected individuals to exhibit unusual behaviors but rather the "Spirit of God" that inspired the whole community. Without that particular Spirit, no one in the community could accept the one truth necessary for salvation: "Jesus is Lord." On the other hand, no one endowed with that Spirit could ever curse Jesus, because that would be a contradiction in terms: the Spirit came from the Father and from Jesus (1 Corinthians 12:1-3).

Truly, the gift of the Spirit of God so unites the whole community that no one can stand out as "special" or distinct from the others. The community exists as a community of faith only because the Spirit of God has enabled all of them to believe in Jesus.

Once Paul raised the issue of the Spirit, however, more needed to be said. The basic problem with the church in Corinth was that it was not acting like a community. Members of the congregation divided into splinter groups. Each formed itself on the basis of their allegiance to certain individuals. "'I belong to Paul,' or 'I belong to Apollos,' or 'I belong to Cephas,' or 'I belong to Christ'" (1 Corinthians 1:12).

Each group apparently emphasized their spiritual ancestry above the Spirit who gathered them. How could Paul define a centripetal force to hold them together? What would unite these separated groups into a community?

The answer was obvious for a church created by the outpouring of the Holy Spirit on the Day of Pentecost. If the Spirit united people of many lands and languages by enabling them to hear God's Word, then that same Spirit was the centripetal force that would keep them together despite their differences.

Their differences were many. Like any other community, this one included people who had different gifts, different forms of ministry, and different abilities. Yet, instead of separating groups on the basis of these differences, they were meant to be one fully equipped community. They all received their gifts from the same Spirit. They all served the same Lord, Jesus Christ. They all worked with the talents given by the same God. One Spirit, one Lord, one God made them one community!

Paul's emphasis here is a far cry from the way the Corinthians had divided themselves. Special interest groups or cliques had no valid place in a Spirit-filled community. On the contrary, the richly varied gifts of the Spirit enabled differently-gifted persons to serve the common good.

Yet Paul did not sweep their differences under the proverbial rug. In fact, the common good is served by their differences. The Spirit of God conveys to some in the community "...the utterance of wisdom, to others the utterance of knowledge...faith...gifts of healing...the working of miracles... prophecy...the ability to distinguish between spirits...various kinds of tongues..." and even "the interpretation of tongues" (12:8-10). In community, the strength of one becomes the strength of all.

Fast Facts

◆ Corinth, a Greek city not far from Athens, was visited by Paul on his second missionary journey (Acts18).
◆ *Ecstasy* means literally "outside of oneself."
◆ Apollos, a common Greek name because of a major god by that name, was a highly educated Jewish Christian from Alexandria in Egypt.
◆ *Cephas* was another name for the apostle Peter.

To explain how this works, Paul compares the church to a human body. Our physical bodies consist of many parts. Each part serves a specific function. The eyes see, the ears hear, the mouth speaks, the hands touch, the feet walk. No part can exclude itself because it functions differently than another. The body needs each and all of its parts working together.

In the same way, Paul wrote, the church is the body of Christ. Each part is different, each serves a different function, each has a different talent, but together we all make up the one body that is the church.

We belong to the body of Christ because we are all baptized in the one Spirit. We become whole—not in spite of our differences, but through them.

GALATIANS 5:1-26
THE FRUITS OF THE SPIRIT

Christians have some unique views of freedom. What you are free *from* and what you are free *for* become key issues for someone who has been baptized and endowed with the Holy Spirit.

The apostle Paul wrote a letter to the Galatians in order to help them preserve the freedom he had shown them several years earlier. When he first met them, he preached what the Spirit sent him to preach: the gospel of Jesus Christ. He told them how Jesus died on the cross to secure their freedom from sin and death. He told them of the resurrection of Jesus and the hope of life to come. Accepting that message of good news in faith was all that was necessary to become God's children.

After Paul had left the scene, however, another group of preachers came along. They insisted Paul's teaching lacked certain necessary rules and rituals. They convinced recently converted Christians they must follow the regulations of Jewish law, including circumcision, if they hoped to be saved. What does all that have to do with the Spirit of God? Everything!

In the first place, their life as Christians began with the gift of the gospel of Jesus Christ, a gift sealed by the Holy Spirit in baptism (Galatians 3:2). Furthermore the same God who gave the Spirit in the first place is the one who keeps supplying the Spirit and keeps changing lives (3:5). To make the gift conditional on successfully following a host of rules and regulations is contrary to that gift.

For Paul the belief that a human being was saved by the things that he or she does was a totally different idea than the gospel of grace. He called that approach "law," and contrasted it throughout this letter with "gospel." The law is what humans attempt to accomplish. The gospel is what God promises and then actually accomplishes for us.

The law serves certain purposes: it measures how far we have fallen from God, and restrains us from falling deeper into chaos. The law, however, is not good for making us right with God. Only God can do that.

God sets us right through the death and resurrection of Jesus Christ. God fills the baptized community with the Spirit precisely so that it does not rely on itself and its own deeds, but rejoices in what God has done and keeps doing.

If the community of faith adds rules to the gospel, Paul writes, it is throwing away freedom only to enslave itself once again to standards and quotas it cannot fulfill. And so begins chapter 5 with this unambiguous plea: "For freedom Christ has set us free. Stand firm, therefore, and do not submit again to a yoke of slavery" (verse 1).

Paul goes on to illustrate the seriousness of their temptation to require circumcision. Second, he explains that freedom brings with it responsibility.

As for the seriousness of insisting on circumcision, Paul tells his readers that such a condition literally defeats the gospel. The gospel is the good news about the death and resurrection of Jesus Christ. It is free to anyone who will take it, and the Spirit enables people to do so. Adding any condition, no matter how pious it might seem, tells God, "Thanks, but no thanks! I can take care of myself."

Endowed with the Spirit, however, people of faith look forward to more of God's gift. "For through the Spirit, by faith, we eagerly wait for the hope of righteousness" (5:5). That righteousness is not what we do. It is God's righteousness that will save us from sin and death and take us to live in God's kingdom forever.

The first thing Paul writes about freedom, then, is the danger of losing it by imposing a slavish devotion to useless practices. The second thing is what people of faith are free for.

What counts, Paul wrote, is not circumcision or law but "faith working through love" (5:6). Here are two words of supreme significance: faith and love. Faith is not simply intellectual assent or an emotional reaction. Neither is it clinging to a set of rules. Faith is active trust in God who has done everything for us. Trust expresses itself in works of love.

As for *love*, the word can mean several things. It can be the love that people share with one another in a family and among friends. In the Greek, the language in which the New Testament was written, that word is *philia*; it occurs in the name of William Penn's city, Philadelphia, the city of brotherly love. Love can also mean "romance" or "desire." The Greek word is *eros*, the name of a Greek god who was known in ancient Rome as Cupid. We get the word *erotic* from that ancient term.

When Paul writes about "faith working through love," however, he uses a different word entirely: *agape*. It means sacrificing love, serving love, and it is unconditional love. It is *agape* that is used in John 3:16: "For God so loved the world...." Jesus used *agape* when he said, "Love one another, as I have loved you." Agape is the unconditional love of God. Agape is the self-sacrificing love of Jesus Christ. Agape is the love that Jesus commands that people of faith give one another. Agape is the love that faith works through when the Spirit-filled community asserts its God-given freedom to love without expectation of reward.

The only slavery that can result from agape is the voluntary, mutual enslavement of Christians to one another: "through love become slaves to one another" (5:13). That kind of love can only be experienced in a community where differences among people do not count, a community where "there is no longer Jew or Greek, there is no longer slave or free, there is no longer male and female; for all of you are one in Christ Jesus" (Galatians 3:28).

Love ensures that Christians do not take their freedom as an opportunity to do whatever they please. As members of a community gathered by the Holy Spirit, Christians are called to love one another, willingly limiting themselves for the well being of all. This is the meaning of being slaves to one another.

The choice the Christians in Galatia faced, Paul wrote, was whether to walk by the Spirit or by the flesh. They stood at the fork in the road. One sign pointed the way to "the desires of the flesh." It was a path filled with chaos, and it was paved with works of destruction (see the long list in 5:19-21). The other sign pointed to "the Spirit." Along this fruitful path grows "love, joy, peace, patience, kindness, generosity, faithfulness, gentleness, and self-control" (verses 22-23). It was a path of harmony on which freedom had not been abused but fulfilled.

Rightly, then, Paul urged his readers, "If we live by the Spirit, let us also be guided by the Spirit" (5:25). By doing so, we live by faith and hope in a community of love.

Focus on the Stories
BODY PARTS
The image of the church as the body of Christ makes every member significant. Each baptized member contributes his or her talent to the functioning of the whole body. As you imagine the anatomy of the human body, with which part do you identify yourself? What happens to the body if you do not function? How does the imagery enable you to value other members?

UNITY IN DIVERSITY

The unity of the church is accomplished through the Holy Spirit in the preaching of the gospel and in the administering of the sacraments. What kinds of diversity are evident in your congregation? Are some kinds of diversity not allowed? Should they be allowed?

USE OR ABUSE

Freedom is a wonderful privilege, whether we use that term as citizens of our country or as members of the church. How can we in either of those areas prevent the abuse of freedom so that it becomes a license to do whatever each of us chooses?

CHAOS VERSUS ORDER

The list of vices at Galatians 3:19-21 represents the path of chaos. Do you think the entire list is important? Do you think some are worse than others? Review the fruits of the Spirit at 3:22-23. Do you consider some to be more significant than others? Do you think it is important that the first "fruit" on the list is love?

For the Next Session

While we have studied the activity and purpose of the Holy Spirit in our lives here and now, what role does the Spirit have for us in the future reign of God?

Closing

O Holy Spirit, bind
Our hearts in unity
And teach us how to find
The love from self set free;
In all our hearts such love increase;
That every home, by this release
May be the dwelling place of peace.

—F. B. Tucker
(*Lutheran Book of Worship* #357)

A View from the Mountain

The Holy Spirit raises our view to see beyond the present to God's eternal reign.

REVELATION 21:1-11; 22:17
THE NEW CREATION

Toward the end of the first century, Domitian, the emperor of Rome, renewed the persecutions of Christians that delighted some of his predecessors. Among the people he had sent into exile was the man we know as John the Seer. John spent several years on the Greek island of Patmos where the Holy Spirit inspired him to write letters to seven Christian communities. His purpose was to offer them hope in their difficult times and to challenge them to repent.

As John the Seer brought his book to a conclusion, he reported the vision God gave him concerning a new heaven and a new earth. In this new creation all pain and illness, even death itself, will cease to exist.

Then the Spirit took him up on a high mountain and showed him the heavenly city of Jerusalem, the bride, coming down out of heaven from God. What he saw was a vision of God's glorious kingdom that represented the opposite of what assaulted his sight every day. This vision of hope was not meant for John's eyes alone. "The Spirit and the bride say, 'Come'" (Revelation 22:17). In that invitation, the Spirit conveys the hospitality of God to all who look to God in trust.

Focus on the Stories

INTIMACY AND LIFE

When we studied the story of creation in Genesis 2, we read that God breathed into Adam's nostrils in order to make him alive. How does the vision of the new creation in Revelation reflect the kind of intimacy we studied in the first creation?

VISIONING THE END TIME

The prophecy from the book of Joel looked forward to the Day of the Lord when God would pour out the Spirit on all flesh. We studied about the Day of Pentecost in Acts 2 where Peter quoted that particular passage from Joel to indicate the Day of the Lord had arrived. How does the passage from Revelation 21–22 connect with those earlier passages? Is it a difficult connection to make?

THE ULTIMATE TEACHER

When we studied the Gospel of John, we focused on various roles Jesus said the Holy Spirit would play. Do you recall them? (Review Session 4 if needed.) Here in Revelation 21–22, the Spirit functions as the one who leads John to the place he sees the vision. Is that function consistent with any of those roles from John's Gospel?

BRINGING HOME THE VISION

How can the vision of the new creation (Rev. 21–22) comfort you in hard times or cause a difference in the way you live? Could it affect your congregation's life and ministry? As you respond, consider implications Paul listed for a Spirit-endowed faith community.

Closing

And as we are strangers and pilgrims on earth, help us to prepare for the world to come, doing the work which you have called us to do while it is day, before that night comes when no one can work. And, when our last hour shall come, support us by your power and receive us into your everlasting kingdom, where, with your Son our Lord Jesus Christ and the Holy Spirit, you live and reign, God forever. Amen

—Service of the Word (*Lutheran Book of Worship,* pp. 129-130)

How the Bible Is Organized

The Bible is divided into two "testaments." The Old Testament, which was originally written in Hebrew, contains four major sections that include 39 individual books. The New Testament, which was originally written in Greek, is divided into three sections that include 27 books.

THE OLD TESTAMENT

The Pentateuch
Genesis
Exodus
Leviticus
Numbers
Deuteronomy
History
Joshua
Judges
Ruth
1 and 2 Samuel
1 and 2 Kings
1 and 2 Chronicles
Ezra
Nehemiah
Esther
Wisdom
Job
Psalms
Proverbs

Ecclesiastes
Song of Solomon
Prophets
Isaiah
Jeremiah
Lamentations
Ezekiel
Daniel
Hosea
Joel
Amos
Obadiah
Jonah
Micah
Nahum
Habakkuk
Zephaniah
Haggai
Zechariah
Malachi

THE NEW TESTAMENT

The Gospels
Matthew
Mark
Luke
John
History
Acts of the Apostles
The Letters
Romans
1 and 2 Corinthians
Galatians
Ephesians

Philippians
Colossians
1 and 2 Thessalonians
1 and 2 Timothy
Titus
Philemon
Hebrews
James
1 and 2 Peter
1, 2, and 3 John
Jude
Revelation

Adapted from *A Beginner's Guide to Reading the Bible* by Craig R. Koester, copyright © 1991 Augsburg Fortress.

How to Read the Bible

FINDING A BIBLE REFERENCE

1. Check the Bible's table of contents if you do not know where the book is.

PSALM 119:105
book of Bible   chapter   verse

2. In your Bible, the chapter numbers are large numbers, usually at the beginning of paragraphs. The chapter numbers might also be printed at the top of each page.
3. The verse numbers are tiny numbers, usually printed at the beginning of sentences.

UNDERSTANDING WHAT YOU READ

As you read a passage of the Bible, keep in mind these three questions:
1. What does this text tell me about God?
2. What does this text tell me about the people of God?
3. What does this text tell me about myself?

GOING DEEPER

Other questions that might help you understand what you are reading include:
1. What type of literature is this passage? Is it a story? A historical account? Poetry? A hymn? A letter? How might that affect my understanding of the passage?
2. What is the historical situation of the writer?
3. Who is speaking in this passage?
4. Who is being addressed in this passage? How am I like or different from that person or group?
5. How does the passage relate to the surrounding text? Does the surrounding material shed any light on the passage's meaning?
6. What are the key words and phrases in the passage? Which ones do I not understand?
7. How does the passage compare to parallel passages or to texts on the same subject?
8. What in the passage puzzles, surprises, or confuses me?

"Going Deeper" is adapted from *Bible Reading Handbook* by Paul Schuessler, copyright © 1991 Augsburg Fortress.

Luther Says . . .

I. GOD'S WORK AS FATHER/CREATOR

The first article [of the Creed] teaches that God is the Father, the creator of heaven and earth. What is this? What do these words mean? The meaning is that I should believe that I am God's creature, that he has given to me body, soul, good eyes, reason, a good wife, children, fields, meadows, pigs, and cows, and besides this, he has given to me the four elements, water, fire, air, and earth. Thus this article teaches that you do not have your life of yourself, not even a hair. I would not even have a pig's ear, if God had not created it for me. Everything that exists is comprehended in that little word "creator." Here we could go on preaching at length about how the world, which also says, I believe in God, believes this. Therefore everything you have, however small it may be, remember this when you say "creator," even if you set great store by it. Do not let us think that we have created ourselves, as the proud princes think.

Luther's Works, vol. 51, Sermons I, edited and translated by John W. Doberstein (Philadelphia: Fortress Press, 1959), 162-163.

II. CHRIST'S WORK

On Galatians 2:19, "For I through the Law died to the Law, that I might live to God."

Thus with the sweetest names Christ is called my Law, my sin, and my death, in opposition to the Law, sin, and death, even though in fact He is nothing but sheer liberty, righteousness, life, and eternal salvation. Therefore He became Law to the Law, sin to sin, and death to death, in order that He might redeem me from the curse of the Law, justify me, and make me alive.... Thus Christ is a poison against the Law, sin, and death, and simultaneously a remedy to regain liberty, righteousness, and eternal life.

Luther's Works, vol. 26, Lectures on Galatians, 1535, Chapters 1–4, edited by Jaroslav Pelikan (Saint Louis: Concordia Publishing House, 1963), 163.

III. THE HOLY SPIRIT'S WORK

The third article [of the Creed], therefore, is that I believe in the Holy Spirit, that is, that the Holy Spirit will sanctify me and is sanctifying me.... How does he sanctify me? By causing me to believe that there is one, holy church through which he sanctifies me, through which the Holy Spirit speaks and causes the preachers to preach the gospel. The same he gives to you in your heart through the sacraments, that you may believe the Word and become a member of the church. He begins to sanctify now; when we have died, he will complete this sanctification through both "the resurrection of the body" and "the life everlasting."

Luther's Works, vol. 51, *Sermons I,* edited and translated by John W. Doberstein (Philadelphia: Fortress Press, 1959), 168.

IV. ESCHATOLOGY

The significance of baptism is a blessed dying unto sin and a resurrection in the grace of God, so that the old man, conceived and born in sin, is there drowned, and a new man, born in grace, comes forth and rises.... This significance of baptism—the dying or drowning of sin—is not fulfilled completely in this life.... For sin never ceases entirely while the body lives.... There is no help for the sinful nature unless it dies and is destroyed with all its sin. Therefore the life of a Christian, from baptism to the grave, is nothing else than the beginning of a blessed death. For at the Last Day, God will make him altogether new.

Luther's Works, vol. 35, *Word and Sacrament I,* edited by E. Theodore Bachman (Philadelphia: Fortress Press, 1960) 30-31.

V. FREEDOM OF A CHRISTIAN

Now that the question is raised, we must have a look at the nature of Christian freedom. Christian or evangelical freedom, then, is a freedom of conscience which liberates the conscience from works. Not that no works are done, but no faith is put in them.... Christ has freed this conscience from works through the gospel and teaches this conscience not to trust in works, but to rely only on his mercy....

And so, the conscience of a man of faith depends solely and entirely on the works of Christ. The conscience may be likened to the dove resting in safety in the clefts of the rock and in the secret places [Song of Sol. 2:14]. Such a soul knows with absolute certainty that it can have neither confidence nor peace except in Christ alone, and that in its own works nothing but guilt, fear, and condemnation can abide.

Luther's Works, vol. 44, *The Christian in Society,* edited by James Atkinson (Philadelphia: Fortress Press, 1966), 298-299.